Introduction

As a way of saying *Thanks,* I am offering you this free guide on how to make money online today.

Also, please feel free to check out my blog with content which may help you out with your business.

**Note – The guide is available for download starting with 20th November 2015.

To the download the guide, click right on the photo and it will be delivered to your email after you sign up.

Enjoy!

ONLINE STARTUP

20 ideas to make money online today

Ryan Stevens

Chapter 1: Importance of Launching a Book Properly

Launching a book on Amazon is a complex strategy that takes months to be correctly understood.

For most authors on Amazon, this has been the most challenging process of the business.

How can you launch a book?

1. *Free launch*
2. *Paid launch at $0.99*
3. *Both – Free + Paid*

Most of the scammers and all of the so called 'online entrepreneurs' will tell you that "self-publishing is a passive income stream – you only do it once and then you're *done* – money will start rolling in over and over again, month after month. "

Now let me tell you the sad truth… Everything you heard is completely *WRONG.*

There is no such thing as 100% passive income stream – any kind of business needs maintenance, even passive ones. As a wise person once said, **"If you're not growing, you're dying."**

Once you (successfully) launch a book, after a while, it will start lagging in sales – this means that you will slowly make less and less sales than you would have initially.

So what can you do to improve them and make the book sell again?

1. *Pulse Countdown deals – Run multiple promotions at $0.99 and earn a 70% royalty.*
2. *Pulse Free KDP Select promotion – Set a free promotion to get more*

visibility (more downloads are equal to more potential sales).

Now I'll be completely honest with you – free promos are not as good as paid promotions, but they require more experience, an author platform, and much more. I will discuss this topic in the following chapters.

Chapter 2: The Truth about Self-publishing

Self-publishing is becoming more and more popular these days and it gets harder to keep up with the changes of our modern society and it gets even harder to compete with other publishers.

The truth is this: Only the first 100,000 books sell well on Kindle, from #1 (+5,000 units/day) to #100,000 (~1 unit/day).

Titles ranked from #100,000 to #200,000 sell 1 copy every 2-3 days, depending on the traffic in that day.

Titles above #200,000 barely sell – they don't get into charts, Amazon doesn't promote them, they aren't "Hot New

Releases", and they become dust collectors.

You see, there a lot of courses out there that promote this self-publishing as the Holy Grail. Gurus promote this business as if it was the only online business in the world.

It's a nice place to start an online career, it's something that requires work, commitment, patience, time, and money. You can start this business with no money, but it will be very difficult.

I must admit that I started this business with only $120, but it was 1 year ago when things were easier and I had the luck to start (by mistake) in the best month of the year (for Amazon sales), December.

To stand out of the crowd, you need to do something that few people do – invest, write high quality content, adopt as many strategies as possible, and things will change.

The only way to adopt the best strategy is to keep experiencing. I am going to tell you my whole experience, all my thoughts, everything I know, but you will be the one who is making decisions and you will be the one who will market your books – in your own way.

In other words, you are competing with the first 100,000 books on Amazon.

It's challenging but if you choose the right strategies, you can become a bestseller, and you can make more than $1,000 per month with only 1 title if you apply all the strategies.

Chapter 3: My Experience with Launching Books on Amazon

My very first self-published Kindle book on Amazon was about productivity – ways to improve productivity, ways to achieve success – it had 12,000 words, which was converted into 45 Kindle pages or 74 Print (real) pages.

I must admit that I hadn't written it. I hired a ghostwriter to do that for me, as I was at the "experiment" phase back then.

So, I invested $120 in the content, $20 in multiple covers, I didn't invest in any advertising (I thought that all the websites were scams, but they aren't), and I didn't make more than $20 with it. That happened in December 2014 when I was a complete beginner.

Then guess what? I was frustrated that I lost the money, that my book sucks, that I am not good at this and lots of negative thoughts.

But the truth was different. I wasn't applying the right selling strategy and I didn't launch the book – I just enrolled it into KDP Select, I scheduled it for a free promo of 5 days, and nothing happened. I got like 300-400 downloads for it in 5 days knowing that I had around 3 reviews, of which 2 were from my friends and family.

Not bad, but not good either.

After the promotion ended, I was seeing a sale every 3-4 days and after a month, it completely died.

I tried to change the cover and to change keywords and I've tried to revive it somehow in the following 1-2 months and nothing magical happened. So I finally decided to leave it on my bookshelf and let it collect dust.

I was focusing on my next books and I learned a lot new skills, strategies, etc., and I found a service and a new strategy that was *GOLD* – BuckBooks, a free service (until September 2015) that promoted your book only if it was high quality to an audience that was willing to pay 1 Buck for 1 Book ($0.99).

I had impressive results with my other books and I thought that I can use this service to revive my first book. And so it was.

I submitted it for free, I got 104 purchases at $0.99 in 24 hours and that boosted my book through the rankings – it became a bestseller in 2 categories and after 2-3 days, I was getting organic sales.

So, I made 104 x $0.99 x 0.35 = $36.4 during the promo, for which I didn't pay a dime, and in the following 30 days, I got 800 KENP pages, 55 sales at a full price of $2.99, and 21 paperback sales at $6.99 (I was earning $2.04 for each sale), which converts into $0.0057 x 800 + $36.4 + 55 x $2.07 + $42.84 = $197.65

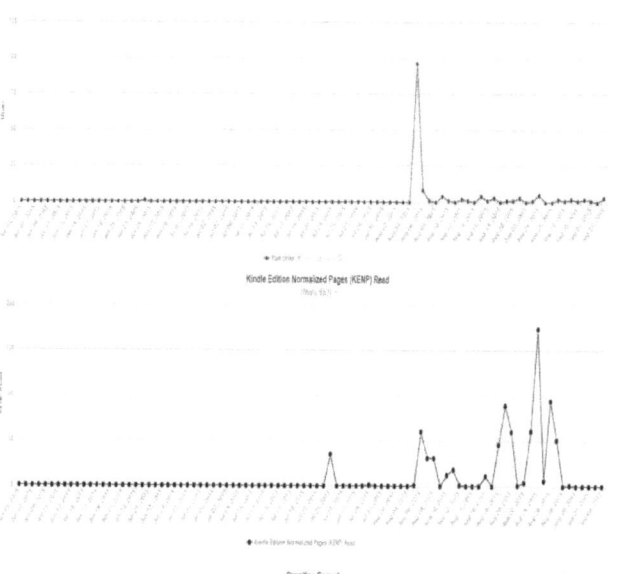

Kindle Edition Normalized Pages (KENP) Read

Royalties Earned

Knowing that I made around $20-30 since I've uploaded the book, plus the amount that I made in the next 30 days, I have managed to get $227.65 and to obtain profit.

That book still makes me money today, I usually sell 1-2 books/day (on average) and I have made in total around $450 (in 1 year).

You know, Amazon's algorithm goes like this: If you upload a new book and you "prove" that your book is good (you make sales, you get a high number of reviews, it's been professionally formatted, edited, it has a professional cover and you have 15,000 – 20,000 words in it (~90-100 Kindle pages ~ 150-170 Print Pages)), then you have a 99% chance to make a killing on Amazon.

If you do what I did, to revive a book after 6-7 months from when it was published, it won't have the same effect. Amazon promotes your book into charts such as "New Hot Releases", "New Releases", "People also bought", "Recommendations", and more.

If you revive a book after a few months like I did, you will lose half of the charts, so half of the sales.

Amazon Associates 1st Launch (June 2015)

Another experience of mine that had incredible results was with Amazon Associates book, my first book on my official Pen Name (Ryan Stevens).

I wrote it entirely by myself, it has around 13,000 words I think – it has 100 pages (print) and it had 60 pages in the Kindle format.

I spent 3 weeks writing it, I ordered a professional cover, I sent it to proofreading to correct any commas or errors and then I did a mixed launch (Free + Paid).

I must admit that I had luck.

I paid DigitalBookToday ($15), BKnights ($5.5 – Fiverr), eBookshabit (10$), and Fussy Librarian ($8), and I got 2,200 downloads. That also brought me 11 organic reviews 2 of three stars, 4 of 4 stars, 1 of 1 star, and the rest were 5 stars.

Soon after the free promo, I submitted my book to BuckBooks – I made 141 sales in 1 day and then everything exploded.

My best rank was #1621 (see picture) and I was a bestseller in 3 categories.

Amazon Best Sellers Rank: #1,621 Paid in Kindle Store (See Top 100 Paid in Kindle Store)
  #1 in Kindle Store > Kindle eBooks > Business & Money > Accounting
  #1 in Kindle Store > Kindle eBooks > Business & Money > Marketing & Sales > Advertising
  #1 in Kindle Store > Kindle eBooks > Business & Money > Marketing & Sales > Marketing > Web Marketing

After 3 days, the book was making 10 – 16 sales per day at $2.99.

To sum up, I have invested $83.50 in the book:

- $20 cover (print ready)
- $25 proofreading
- $38.5 in free advertising
- $0 in BuckBooks ($0.99 launch)

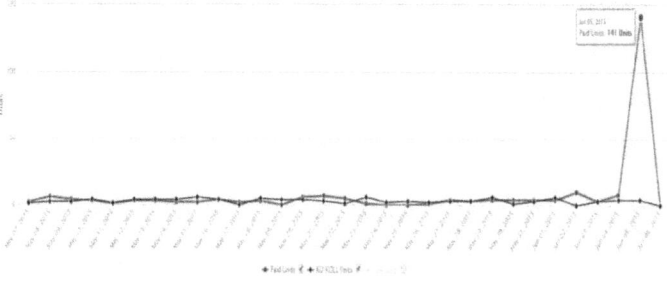

I made $49.35 during the BuckBooks feature and then I was averaging 8 – 14 sales per day, 4 to 8 borrows (at $1.35 per borrow – before 1st July 2015), and 1 paperback sale every 1-2 days (I made 19 in the next 30 days).

So I was making $20 - $30/day with one single book. I have earned $680 in 30 days including the launch feature + the paperback sales.

I was amazed by the results and I have continued to use this method.

Amazon Associates 2nd Launch (September 2015)

I wasn't able to use BuckBooks again – they allow you to use it every 6 months for the same title and once per week (the same author).

So I decided to run a free promo and to invest $160 just in free advertising. I was expecting around 4,000 - 5,000 downloads and the result – a huge disappointment.

I have read on a blog that if you manage to generate +5,000 downloads and then to drop the price down to $0.99, you could expect 30-70 sales a day at $0.99 and then 20-40 sales a day at $2.99.

I guess that person was right, but the problem with my launch is that I just made 850 free units.

I was disappointed because I have invested $38.50 at the beginning and had great results (with small sites), and then when I invested in bigger sites and 4 times more money, I got 50% less downloads.

I was really disappointed.

What I learned from this:

1. Amazon traffic varies from month to month.
2. Don't promote a book when it's an official free day or an event (such as Labor Day in the US).
3. Results are always different.

Overall, the Amazon Associates book did a great job over months – I have invested around $220 in it and I have generated over $1,400; $680 in the first month, $250 in the second month, and then I have been steadily making $100-$150 per month from KDP and $20 - $50/month from CreateSpace.

I am sure that I could've made more if Amazon wouldn't have changed the KU system – in the first month, I made around $190 just from borrows alone, in the second month, I made only $28.

I will promote this book every 6 months via Kindle Countdown Deal at $0.99 through multiple platforms for the best results and I quit promoting books for free – a waste of time, money, patience, etc.

Note – I am sorry if the images are blurry, as you see, the screenshots were taken back in June-July when the old KU system was available. I tried as much as possible to make them visible.

Kindle Publishing PRO Launch

I have launched this book at the end of June 2015 and I have used the same method – Free launch followed by Paid launch.

The book was written by me, and it contains screenshots and a very detailed process – from writing, to advertising + tips. It has 166 pages (print), around 18,000 words and over 30 screenshots. I explain all that I know about this whole process. It's been constantly updated – when I found out something new, I immediately went to update the content.

If you are reading this book and you don't know the whole process, take a look at it:

Kindle Publishing PRO – Complete Expert Guide

I have invested a total of $143.50:

- $20 cover
- $25 - proofreading (failed) – I used a gig for several times called SydneyMorgan on Fiverr for proofreading and that time, she didn't proofread anything. As she has done a great job for my first book, I didn't take a look at the second proofread – big mistake.
- $25 – 2nd proofreading
- $8 – Fussy Librarian
- $5.50 – Fiverr – Bknights
- $50 – BooksButterfly
- $10 – eBookshabit
- $0 – BuckBooks

The results were like this:

- 1,972 free downloads
- 84 units at $0.99 through BuckBooks and then the book

started to make organic sales at $2.99.

- I was averaging 5 sales per day for a month and 2-4 borrows per day. I have only sold 5 paperback copies in the next 30 days.

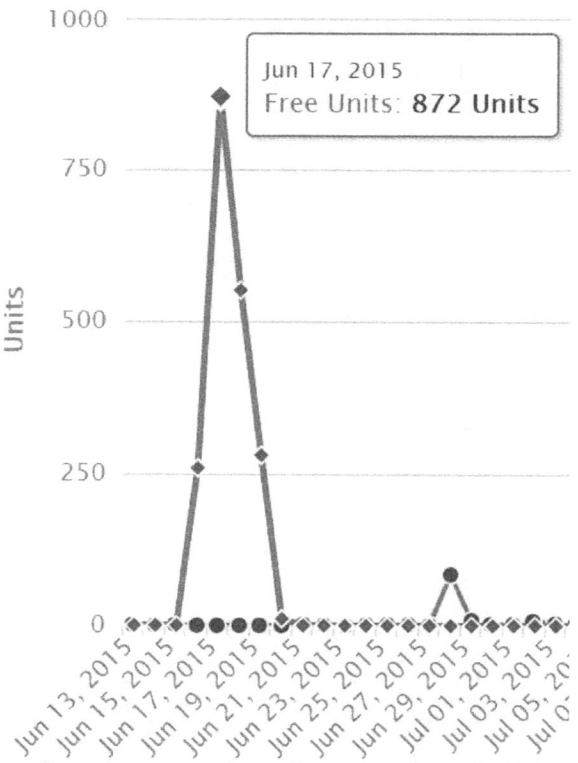

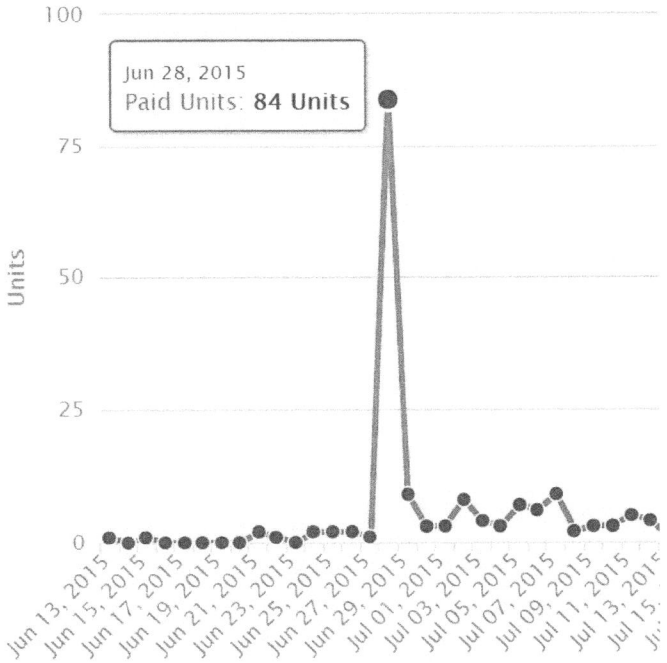

Jun 28, 2015
Paid Units: **84 Units**

I was a little disappointed because I had invested more than I did in my first launch on my Amazon Associates book and got slightly fewer sales and downloads.

Overall, I was happy with the income that the book provided - $300-$350 in the first month (with borrows at $1.35) and then $80 - $120/month.

I have made in total around $600 with this book and I have invested $143. I think it's a great deal knowing that even today, it makes me money (around 1-3 sales a day).

What I learned:

- The sales are influenced 70% by the paid units and 30% by the free units.
- Results are different from book to book.
- The topic has a great influence upon the sales.
- Every books drops in rankings and needs to be promoted again.

Entrepreneur Enhanced Launch

This is the last book for which I have used the Free + Paid strategy.

I initially wanted to wait 30 days to use the Countdown deal, but I changed my mind and I thought that I could get more reviews during a free promo and I realized that it was a mistake.

Free promotions are great at the beginning of your self-publishing career when you have no experience, no platform, no books, and no audience.

As soon as you experience a few launches, you write a few books, and shift to the $0.99 launch, instead of investing $150 like I did initially in a free launch, invest $150 in a paid launch – you get money during the promo, you boost your paid rank, and you get more exposure.

There are lots of benefits, but it's harder to launch. But you know what? Harder is better – everyone uses the free launch, so be a smart author and use a different one.

Entrepreneur Enhanced has 114 pages (print pages) and it's more like a motivational book for those who want to start an online business but they're afraid to fail, they're afraid to start, etc.

I explain what the advantages of the Internet are in our days, I explain a few rules for success, a few tips for productivity, and I talk about my personal life – how I started my own online business, with examples.

I also present a few methods/ideas to make money online.

If you want to know more about it, check this link:

Entrepreneur Enhanced

I have invested a lot of money in this book and the mistake was that I have invested in the worst period – August - September.

I will talk later about the best months for making money with Kindle but right now, I will continue to discuss the results from this book.

I have invested a total of $280.50 as follows:

- $38 in the cover (with a premium stock photo)
- $30 express proofreading
- $50 – BooksButterfly
- $15 – DigitalBookToday
- $15 – BookGoodies
- $15 – Bargainebookhunter
- $3 – Freeebooksdaily
- $10 – eBookshabit
- $10 – Reading Deals
- $5.50 – Fiverr

- $40 – BargainBooksy (at $0.99)
- $49 – BuckBooks (at $0.99 - not free anymore)

Results:

1,100 free units (1,010 were in the US market).

49 units at $0.99 through BuckBooks (below my expectations)

6 units at $0.99 through BargainBooksy – will never use it again.

I am not going to lie to you... this was the worst launch that I have ever made. I have invested over $280 and I got less in return than I got in June for my Associates book, in which I invested only 38$ in.

In 30 days since I launched the book, my numbers are like this – 62 units at $0.99, 14 units at $2.99, 1,167 KENP pages (equivalent to $5.83) and 1 CreateSpace paperback unit ($2.83 royalty). All of these are equal to approximately $57 in revenue. Until I break even to $280, I need a couple of months and patience. I am more than sure that I will make my money back and I will also make profit, but my biggest disappointment was on the short-term.

After promotion

I am proud to say that 99% of the books I've published brought me at least double my money and all of them broke even at some point.

My biggest surprise was from my first book, which during August, September, and October, made me in average 30-40 copies a month at $2.99, +1,000 KENP pages, and around 4-5 copies on CreateSpace. When I initially saw that the book wasn't selling (when I was an absolute newbie), I thought, *Well, I just lost a book, some time, and over $100*, but it proved to be opposite.

I do believe that self-publishing is a great business and it can make you a fortune if you use all the available tools, but unfortunately, it's becoming harder to start or to pursue because of the bad results from KDP Select or from free promotions (this affects fresh-starters).

The reason results for free books are going down?

Too many crappy books with 20 pages from "authors" who have suffocated the market. It's obvious that those people got sick and angry after purchasing or downloading those and whenever they see a free book, they simply don't click on them.

Amazon should do something to improve the quality of the books, they should improve the reviewing process.

I am not saying that my books are the best or they're ultimate quality, I'm just sharing my experience and thoughts for a small fee. I am an indie author, but my aim isn't to scam people with 20 page books, my goal is to grow and to help others grow as well. Scammers don't think like that, they just want to make you click and buy their pamphlets.

If you're willing to make money from Amazon from writing 20 page books with lots of mistakes and you're hoping to make money... please do something else. My book isn't for you and you don't deserve to be called an author or even a publisher. I also hope that you're not trying to "launch" one of those books using the information from this book.

I am encouraging legit people with decent books to grow and start a self-publishing business or an online business.

Evernote Book

I have never had any better results with a book before I launched this book.

The book has 96 pages and it's a step-by-step guide on setting up your Evernote account. It also contains illustrations, tips, and ideas for using the application in a simple and practical manner.

As you would expect, I launched the book at $0.99 and what's even more interesting, I spent a lot less money launching it compared to a free launch.

What I used?

BuckBooks, BKnights (Fiverr), and BooksButterfly, so I paid $49. (BuckBooks), 6$ (BKnights), and $25 BooksButterfly. Proofreading cost me $20 and the cover another $20 (with a premium stock photo from Fotolia included in the price). That totals $120 and I made approximately $140 during launch and 5 days after.

The results look like this:

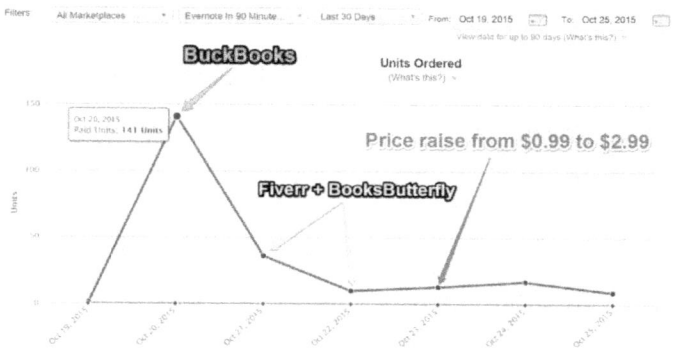

Marketplace	Royalty
Amazon.com	121.35 USD
Amazon.co.uk	1.45 GBP
Amazon.de	0.58 EUR
Amazon.fr	0.33 EUR
Amazon.es	0.00 EUR
Amazon.it	0.00 EUR
Amazon.nl	0.00 EUR
Amazon.co.jp	0.00 JPY
Amazon.in	0.00 INR
Amazon.ca	3.15 CAD
Amazon.com.br	0.00 BRL
Amazon.com.mx	0.00 MXN
Amazon.com.au	5.06 AUD

Generate a detailed royalty report for sales between **October 19, 2015** and **October 25, 2015**

To be honest, I didn't expect these results, but they came as pleasant surprise. After I made almost 200 units in 3 days at $0.99, Amazon's trigger pointed out that my book is selling well and it should be promoted even more.

Should I mention that I was a bestseller in all three categories at $0.99 with a rank of #1,500 and a rank of #6,000-#7,000 while the price was raised at $0.99?

The other books I promoted from June to October (except Associates) didn't perform as well and that's because they didn't reach this number (200 sales in 3 days).

After the promotion, I was making 10-15 sales a day at full price ($2.99), so I was averaging $20-$30 a day just from this book.

Now let's imagine how everything can grow even more if I would have had an email list, a bigger audience, and I would have invested a lot more money. If I could have generated 500 sales in 4-5 day, I would probably have reached a bestseller rank below #800 and I would have made 40-50 sales a day at full price.

Most of the publishers promote their books using KDP Select free days, but that just doesn't work well anymore.

Conclusion of My Experiments

1. *Free promos aren't as effective as $0.99 launches.*

2. *Free promos don't bring you money during the promotions and they don't guarantee anything after.*

3. *Free promos attract people who have no interest in buying your book and this may result in receiving more negative reviews.*

4. *Free books are suffocating Amazon, especially with 'scamphlets', and make people avoid downloading them.*

5. *Free promotions take a lot more time to do compared to a $0.99 launch.*

6. *The topic of a book has a great influence on multiple advertising websites – sometimes if you don't make any sales, it's not because the website sucks, it's because your topic is inadequate.*
7. *Free promotions are good only if you are launching your first 1-2 books and you don't have any idea of what I am saying here.*
8. *Running free promos will eliminate most of your possible customers who would have bought your book anyway.*
9. *Free promotions will make your competitors download it and leave a negative review.*
10. *Paid promotions at $0.99 simply give a better momentum to books and you can break even on your investment a lot faster. (Just check out my last launch again).*

Chapter 4: 23 Self-publishing Strategies

Now, let me tell you about those strategies that can turn your self-publishing business into a 6-figure success.

Strategy #1

Choose only one topic/niche.

If you want to build a business and not to self-publish books just as a "hobby" or a "part-time" job, you need to choose 1 topic.

The best topic that you can choose is the one you have a passion for. You need to find a topic that you have knowledge about – let your experience do the work for you.

Strategy #2

Use the #10,000 rule

Look at the bestseller's rank in the category in which you want to enter. If the #1 book in that category (or subcategory) is #10,000 or less, it means that there is market for that book and you have a great chance of making money with your future book.

Strategy #3

Build an author platform.

Write multiple books on the same topic (or for the same audience) and create an authority for yourself.

Use only one Pen Name – Create an Amazon Author Central account, so people can follow you easily.

Every new book that you release will promote your other books.

Strategy #4

Create a blog dedicated to your self-publishing business.

Upload content each week, purchase a premium theme, customize your blog, and include links in your books to the blog.

By gaining traffic, you have the possibility to send that traffic to your books on Amazon and you can use it for other strategies, too.

Strategy #5

Build an email list.

As soon as you are done with your blog, sign up with Aweber and create an email list.

Use this list to launch a new book or when you have any seasonal promotions.

That list can be used also for affiliate marketing purposes.

The Aweber service costs from $19/month with the first month free and you can earn commissions by becoming an affiliate. Most of the people who use this end up using it for free and some even earn money from using it (from commissions).

Strategy #6

Offer things for free.

People like free stuff. Give them something for free and make them sign up to your blog and email list.

I also signed up with lots of blogs and websites who use this method. Why not to take advantage of free content, seasonal promotions, and offers?

Maybe you find something that you really need for a low price or even for free.

Strategy #7

Create a free Podcast.

This is a unique way to drive traffic to your blog, enlarge your email list, and reach more readers.

Make an episode each week of 3 to 5 minutes in which you talk about random subjects about the topic that you write about.

When you will be having an audience, people will ask you things that you can then talk about in your Podcast.

You can use this Podcast to launch your book. At the end of your episode, you can say something like, "By the way, my final book is ready and it's only $0.99 for 3 days until the end of the week. Check it out and if you find it helpful, grab your copy before the price goes up."

Strategy #8

Create a Facebook Page and drive traffic to it.

This will also help you add buttons to your blog and your website/blog will rank higher in the Alexa rank (You will get more exposure and more traffic).

Strategy #9

Sign up to multiple social media platforms.

Create a business name or use your blog's name and sign up to multiple social media platforms.

Share your thoughts, posts, and content across all the platforms to gain maximum exposure.

Strategy #10

Create a YouTube channel.

Not only do you have a great opportunity to increase your traffic, to enlarge your audience, but you can also add affiliate links in the description and make money with Google AdSense.

Strategy #11

Launch your books at $0.99.

This is the most powerful tool ever. The free launch is getting weaker and weaker and everyone is using that. Use a smarter way of promoting your books via a paid launch.

The recipe goes like this:

Write your book – Make sure to have at least 12,000 words (60 Kindle pages/100 print pages).

Edit and proofread your book – Pay attention to details unless you want to get negative reviews.

Upload your book – Upload your book on KDP and on CreateSpace at the same time.

Get reviews – Organic, friends and family, send your book to Goodreads, ask top reviewers from Amazon to have a look at your book, use Amazon's reviewing services, etc. There are dozens of ways that can bring you legit reviews to your book. Just in case you haven't heard, Amazon sued 1,114 people (mainly from Fiverr) who were "selling" fake reviews.

The more reviews you get in a shorter period of time, the higher your book ranks.

Let everyone know about your new release

Tell your audience (blog, YouTube, Facebook, friends, other social media platforms, Podcast, and email list) about your new release.

If you have a medium sized email list (5,000 – 10,000 subscribers) and a decent blog, you should be able to generate 100-500 sales at $0.99 in 1-2 days.

Spread multiple promotions across 5 days

Amazon wants to see that your new release is selling good. To prove that, you need to generate at least 50 sales a day at $0.99 for 5 days.

Invest

Prepare to invest around $200 - $300 if you want to make $1,000 in the first month.

Invest in services such as:

- BuckBooks
- BooksButterfly
- BKnights

- (Fiverr)
- eBookshabit
- eBooklister
- BookBub
- EreaderNewsToday
- DigitalBookToday
- BookGoodies
- Freeebooksdaily
- BookGorilla
- Genre Pulse
- AuthorMarketingClub
- BargainBooksy
- BookSends
- Kboards

Strategy #12

Save/Track results from each book launch and compare them.

Every book launch is different. The audience is different, the content is different, the cover is different, everything is different, and so your results will vary.

Create a chart or a spreadsheet with all the promotions that you used for your book launch and always use the best services.

I can't tell you which are the best promotional websites because it varies – fiction or nonfiction, romance or science fiction, dog training or horse riding. Topics are different and you never know what subscribers from each website want.

For me, the best promotional services were BuckBooks and BooksButterfly (for nonfiction/how-to books)

Strategy #13

Find a co-author to work with.

Try to find an author who writes on the same topic as you and try to contact him.

By working with someone who has experience and an audience, you will increase your sales and visibility. Your partner will take advantage of your audience and you will take advantage of his.

Strategy #14

Re-launch books every 6 months at $0.99.

It's no secret that every Kindle book will drop in rankings at some point.

So don't give it away for free, run promotions (preferably different from the ones used in the launch process) and run a Kindle Countdown Deal.

Strategy #15

Re-launch multiple books using Countdown Deal at the same time.

Find an appropriate period of the year when you should run a Countdown Deal on most of your titles (such as Christmas).

Strategy #16

Work on a daily basis.

Don't procrastinate because your business will suffer and then you will suffer.

Schedule your tasks, outsource what is time consuming, and focus on growth.

Strategy #17

Be patient.

Results won't come overnight, so "keep calm and work" until results will come.

This business is one of the easiest to get started, even though it becomes harder to generate 6 or 7 figures.

Strategy #18

Use PPC Ads.

This is a profitable long-term strategy for growing your audience and income, and for boosting your rank.

You can set ads at Amazon (Amazon Marketing Campaigns), Facebook, Goodreads, and Google.

The most profitable seemed to be Facebook and Goodreads. Amazon is the least profitable, but it depends on the niche, cover, title, number of reviews, etc.

Strategy #19

Create a free course on Udemy.

You only need a microphone to get started and a recording software (Camtasia, for example). For those who have this piece of software, you need to record the screen of your computer when it's in a PowerPoint presentation with a step-by-step course. There's no need to record yourself or to create something complex at the beginning.

From there, you can target people to your blog, books, email list, or on your social media accounts.

Strategy #20

Publish perma-free books (more about how to set up a perma-free book later).

One way to reach more readers is to upload a couple of books for free (usually the start of a series). I have written a book called *Laptop Buying Guide* that I want to set for free permanently. The purpose of the book is to help people choose a laptop depending on what they do – you're a 40 year old man who doesn't need too much, so here's a type of laptop (examples, prices, specs, etc.); you're an entrepreneur - here's another type of laptop; you're a writer or a publisher - here's another type of laptop; you travel a lot - here's another laptop and the list goes on and on.

Perma-free books will generate around 20 – 100 free units per day (let's say 50 on average), so that would be 1,500 per month.

If we convert that to a 1% sales of the other books, that results to 15 sales for the other books you have. Also, there's a 10-20% conversion ratio for the number of subscribers to your email list on your blog (if you put links to your blog there). That equates to 100-300 new subscribers per month.

You can publish your perma-free book on other platforms (Apple, Kobo, Nook, SmashWords, etc.) and you will make subscribers from there, too.

This type of books should have around 4,000-7,000 words (30-40 Kindle pages, 60-70 print pages).

Strategy #21

Publish books at $0.99 (permanently).

Publish this kind of books without enrolling in KDP Select and publish it on other platforms to get royalties.

This books should have around 7,000-8,000 words (40-50 Kindle Pages, 70-80 print pages).

The purpose of this books is to attract people who read your perma-free books or who want to find out more about a specific niche at a low price.

In other words, it's best to have a portfolio of books from $0.00 to $9.99 if possible. There will always be people who like your work and are willing to pay more to know more, and there will always be people who will hate you no matter what you write about.

Strategy #22

Outsource what you can.

Time is money, so use that wisely. Try to give tasks to other freelancers to help you out with your business (proofreading, promoting on different websites, cover creation, formatting, writing down some ideas, etc.)

No matter how good you are, you can't run this type of business by yourself, you need help.

Strategy #23

Write your books by yourself.

Amazon has full of scammers and "entrepreneurs" who just want to make money overnight from 10 page pamphlets.

99% of those pamphlets are written by ghostwriters or by freelancers who simply rewrite existing content from the Internet. I am not saying that it's something fraudulent, but it may be useless to most of the readers.

What I am saying is to write your books on your own and put the experience that you have in your books. In this way, your book will be unique and will stand in front of others.

Chapter 5: How to Perfectly Launch a Book

This is probably the most important aspect of a book. You need to do a lot of things that matter when you launch a book. But what makes it sell is the initial momentum, which needs an artificial boost.

This will determine the lifetime of your book and its selling potential. So take each of the following steps into consideration:

1. High quality content - Write about a great topic, proofread your content, edit the book, and format it. Make sure to write at least 100 pages for whatever you write.

2. Come up with a great title - A good title needs 2 things: First, to sound good and catch readers' attention and second, that it includes keywords in it.

3. Get a great cover - Pro level covers cost over $100. To be honest, my budget for a cover is around $50, but I will increase the quality. When I first started publishing books, I paid $5 for a cover on Fiverr and they did the job. Now, I have higher expectations, so I also increased the price and quality.

4. Write a detailed description - You are allowed to use up to 4,000 characters (around 500-600 words) for the book's description on Kindle. Use as many as possible, include quotes, and small parts of the book.

5. Get reviews - A great book starts to sell after its first 10 reviews. When you have 50, it will sell even better, and after 100 sales, it will explode. Try to get at least 20 reviews (not fake reviews!!!). There are websites who accept to send your book to readers and you will get organic reviews, you can ask your friends to have a look at your book, you can ask a top rated reviewer on Amazon to look at your book or you can go to Goodreads and ask someone to read your book.

If you have a blog or a website, make a deal with your loyal subscribers. Tell them that if they review your book, you will send them another book as a gift. The reviews can be from 1 star "crap" to 5 stars "great read", but make such deals with your followers or subscribers.

6. Choose between a free launch and a $0.99 launch. If you have published at least 3 books under the same pen name and same topic, you can try to launch your book at $0.99. For greater results, bigger profits, and higher demand, I recommend you go with the $0.99. I used to launch my books with the free strategy, but is isn't worth it anymore.

7. Set your promotion 2-3 weeks after you upload the book. Submit your book to multiple websites like BuckBooks, BooksButterfly, Kboards, eBookshabit,

BKnignts, EreaderNewsToday, DigitalBookToday, BookGorilla, Genre Pulse, or Bargainbooksy.

8. Write a blog post about your new release, so people will know about the launch (if you have a blog).

9. Send an email to your list (if you have an email list). This is the key to your publishing success. A list with 10,000 subscribers with 10% conversion rate will purchase 1,000 copies of your book priced at $0.99 and your rank will go to #200-500. You know what they say, the money is in the list.

10. Use your Podcast (if you have one) and let everyone know about your new launch. I've seen bloggers who managed to achieve +100,000 views/downloads of their episodes in 1 year and they started from scratch.

11. Share your launch on social media (pay for advertising that properly).

12. Spread your promotion over 7 days at $0.99 (or over 5 days for free launch). Don't use all the methods in one day, use from 2 to 5 per day.

Example:

Day 1 - Email to subscribers + blogpost + fiverr;
Day 2 - Social media + podcast;
Day 3 - BuckBooks + eBookshabit + bargainbooksy + genre pulse;
Day 4 - BooksButterfly + ENT;
Day 5 - DigitalBookToday + Kboards;
Day 6 - Last chance email;
Day 7 - Organic results. On the 8th day, you can increase the price to $2.99 or more to get the 70% royalty (up to $9.99).

13. Do everything fast - Amazon's algorithms are like this: lots of sales + lots of reviews in a short period = high ranking + visibility. When they see that your book is selling on a daily basis (20+ sales/day), they will start to promote and market your book. They want to make money like you do.

14. Track your results and compare them to other launches.

Create an Excel sheet and write down all your results. Make a graph to see your progress in real-time.

15. Re-promote your book every 3 or 6 months.

No matter what book you have, your ranks will eventually drop – you will experience lagging sales. To revive them, you need to promote your book again (Free downloads or $0.99 sales).

16. Improve and update your book every 6 or 12 months.

Some books (nonfiction ones) that have topics such as applications, manuals, guides, and how-to books will get old and outdated. To get the best from those books, they need minor updates and improvements. Some readers will give you negative reviews about your book about something they really didn't like. You know what they say – in some negative reviews, there's a small nugget of truth. Figure out the mistakes of the book and try to fix them.

17. Build an author platform with books in the same category/niche.

Publishing multiple books under the same name, in the same category, will give you authority in front of others, especially when your books have been published over a year and have over 100 reviews. People will buy your book rather than a book written by a completely new author with no reviews and no platform.

18. Work hard and stop procrastinating.

Time is money, so don't waste it uselessly. Squeeze the best out of a day, keep fit, stay motivated, and work on a daily basis to achieve your goals.

19. Be different with your writing style (try being unique).

Have you ever heard of the 80/20 principle? It's said that books are being written... from books. You will gain knowledge on a lot of subjects, you will outsource other books, but the key element here is to put your personality into the book (80% content, 20% your own ideas and personality). Be different and original to get the best out of a book.

20. Create a print version of your book on CreateSpace.

From the book that you have already written, create a print edition for old school people who prefer to feel the paper rather than a piece of glass from a phone or tablet. It will cost you only to create a cover, which is $30 - $100. The sales from print editions will be 10-20%

of your digital sales, so for every $1,000 that you make on KDP, you will make another $100 with CreateSpace.

21. Create an Audible version on Audible ACX if the book is selling well.

This is another great way to maximize your profits out of your books, but it requires money to produce the audibles. Audio books are becoming popular these days and it's natural to be that way. Why shouldn't you listen to a self-improvement book on your way home or while you are doing other things instead of reading it? It's time saving and a lot more comfortable. Some audio books are free on Amazon or they offer a free trial.

Note – You need to be a US or a UK resident to be able to produce these books (Audible ACX politics – unfortunately, I can't create such books but I would have liked to).

22. Cooperate with other authors.

If you are successful and I am successful, co-writing a new book together will bring us multiple benefits and 50/50 profits.

Co-authoring can have great results and the main advantage is that you are exchanging contacts and subscribers with the other partner.

23. Use Facebook and Amazon Ads (more details in the next chapter)

Chapter 6: Free Launch Strategy

Launching a book can be a complex process for a lot of authors. It was for me at the beginning, too, and I was so angry because I could barely find the information I was looking for. I had to experience it on my own to see what happens.

If you don't have any books right now, you don't have an author platform, and you don't have any experience with self-publishing, then the free launch is the first strategy you should use.

To take advantage of this strategy, you need to be enrolled in the KDP Select program. I must tell you the competition is growing at alarming levels. When KDP launched in 2012, the first publishers made a lot of money with this system. The royalty for 1 borrow was $2, there were less than 2 million eBooks, and everything was nice and relatively easy to start with.

2 years later, in 2014, I got into this business and I was quite pleased with my first results. In my first month of publishing, I made $56 just from an experiment. It was a book about the Paleo Diet, it had 10,000 words (45 Kindle pages), and I was really impressed. So I kept publishing books and I got better and better at this. At that time, a borrow was $1.41 and there were 3 million eBooks. It was December, the best month for buying and selling on Amazon, so everything worked just fine for me.

Guess what strategy I used for that? The free launch, and I didn't pay a penny for advertising. I was able to get 600 downloads for my Paleo Diet, while it had a low number of pages, and wasn't edited by a professional. After the promotion, I was getting from 2 to 5 sales a day and from 1 to 4 borrows a day. Imagine that I made in around 18 days $56. That means

2 sales and 1 borrow a day on average for the whole month. It's not much, but I was amazed by the how quickly I was able to make money.

Right now, in 2015, the royalty for 1 borrow (a fully read borrowed book) is $1.40 for a book that has 220 pages. For books like mine, which have around 120 pages on average, I get less than $0.80 for a borrow and people often don't go through the whole book, they just read a few chapters.

Launching a book using this strategy is also competitive; there are literally too many free books. If you leave a book alone, without investing in it, you will make around 40 to 70 free downloads per day for a nonfiction book. By paying around $100 like I did for some books, you will see somewhere around 1,000 and 2,000 downloads. To start seeing some money, 2,500 units should be your goal.

To reach that number, you need to:

Share your book on Facebook, Twitter, and other social media platforms.

Pay for advertising:

- BooksButterfly
- Fiverr
- Digitalbooktoday
- Ent
- Freebooksy
- Booksends
- Bookgorilla
- Kboards
- Onehundredfreebook
- Bargainebookhunter
- Pixel scroll
- Bookgoodies
- Genre Pulse
- Fussy Librarian
- Ebookshabit
- Reading Deals
- It's write now
- ReadCheaply

- AuthorMarketingClub
- Book Marketing Tools
- Other

After the free launch, price your book at $0.99 and let it sell like that for 5 days.

Better results come at over 5,000 downloads. 2 years ago, the conversion was like this: For every 100 free downloads, you should expect around 1 sale a day. Now, that rate changed to something equivalent to 500 - 750 downloads = 1 sale/day. So 2,500 downloads won't give you more than 5-6/ day at full price. It's very competitive.

Also, some time ago, 1 free unit was equal to 1 paid unit for visibility and exposure. Now, the rate is 8-10 free units = 1 paid unit for visibility. This means that if you had 2,000 free units 2 years ago, you got the visibility of 15,000 - 20,000 units now.

On the other hand, a $0.99 book launch with 300 sales in 7 days is equivalent to a free launch with over 3,000 free units and you get a boost in rankings, so you receive extra visibility and extra chances of making money with that book.

My advice is this: No matter what results you get, if you are willing to start a long-term self-publishing business, do 1-2 free launches your own way, compare the results, and then switch to a $0.99 launch. I have been using the free launch for over 6 months, but it was a lot better 1 year ago.

The sooner you start, the better it is for your business. I wish I started this in 2012, but I am still glad that I started in 2014 and not in 2015.

Chapter 7: My Failed Experiments with Kindle

Success doesn't come without having a couple of failures (or more). In every business, you have get over some obstacles that get in your way.

No matter what you do, you will make mistakes and the only way to keep moving on is to improve yourself and learn from those mistakes.

The same principles apply here. I had dozens of sleepless nights in which I studied and studied facts, results, experiments from others, opinions, etc. I surfed every page, forum, blog, and video regarding this and although I found useful information, it wasn't enough.

What did I have left but to put out my own ideas out there and see what happens?

Experiment #1

I tried to enter the erotica market with a 60 page book. I didn't invest anything in the first erotica book but I didn't make money with it.

Result: I have made around $20 during its lifetime, but the thing that I lost is time.

The book was called *The Girl Next Door*, but the title isn't available anymore.

The erotica market is one of the most profitable on Amazon. If you look at top 100 top chart, you will see that 90% of the books are fiction and over 30% of those are erotica.

Fiction requires imagination, a complex vocabulary, and techniques to entertain the reader and to keep readers focused on the story line. I must admit, I am terrible at writing fiction books, I have never liked reading that kind of book, but I tried to write one on my own.

I didn't make money, but I didn't lose any money with this failed experiment.

Experiment #2

I completely outsourced another erotica book, for which I paid $50, and it had 40 pages.

Result: I didn't make that money back, I made just around $15-$20 with it and mainly from borrows. I think I made 1 or 2 sales during its lifetime, but I made several borrows.

From these 2 erotica books that I wrote, I barely made my money back.

Conclusion: I will never write erotica again and I will never try to outsource a fiction book.

Experiment #3

Launching or promoting multiple books at the same time and with the same advertising websites.

From my experience, it's the worst thing you can do. I did that when I re-promoted my Associates book and when I launched the Entrepreneur Enhanced book. I used exactly the same websites (which once worked) and I had terrible results for both books.

What I mean 'at the same time' is that I paid for all the service in 1 day for both book, even if there was a 1-2 day gap between them.

If I would have promoted only 1 book and I would have seen the bad results with the services, I would have done the same thing for the next book.

Result: I had low results (see previous chapter with book launching), no major increase in sales, and I lost over $200.

You know what the definition of an entrepreneur is, right?

"Entrepreneur = a person who sets up a business or multiple businesses who takes financial risks in the hope of obtaining profits." - Google

That's what I do and what you have to do to achieve success with any business – to keep trying and experimenting new things.

Conclusion: I will wait to see results for each individual launch or experiment. If the results are positive, I will repeat the process and I will consider improving it.

Experiment #4

Outsourcing a nonfiction book from start to finish – cover, content, proofreading, and formatting.

I have invested $120 in my first book and I completely outsourced it on *iWriter.com.* I have used a premium writer and I was lucky to get outstanding content. It had a few mistakes, but I was really pleased with my investment.

I paid $15 for the cover – In return, I received a Kindle 2D flat cover and a 2D cover for CreateSpace (back+spine+cover).

I didn't invested in advertising, I used free services (including BuckBooks, which was free until 1st September 2015).

Result: Positive – Made profit 2 to 3 times from that book.

Conclusion: I am not the kind of guy who wants to outsource the whole business or a whole book, but when I will be out, ill, on vacation, or I simply don't have the time to finish a project, I will consider hiring a professional ghostwriter. All I have to do is to give him the ideas, keywords, and explain what I want.

Outsourcing an entire book is profitable for nonfiction books, but not for fiction ones.

This was an experiment that didn't fail but I won't use it again too soon.

Experiment #5

I have simply found out that promoting all the books by myself can be a painful and time consuming task to do. So I thought that hiring a virtual assistant to promote my books on social media platforms and on multiple websites would be a great idea.

Of course, I had to explain to him 5 times what I want so he can properly understand what I meant to say.

Result: Nothing changed after he promoted my books on multiple groups and free websites so I fired him. I paid him $20 for each promotion just to submit my book to 20-30 groups and 10-15 websites.

Conclusion: Virtual assistants are okay, but not for what I told him to do. A virtual assistant should handle other tasks.

Chapter 8: Facebook and Amazon Ads

Pay extra attention to this chapter because it can change your whole business (positively). Advertising is sometimes difficult and it requires hard work, attention to detail, a proper strategy, luck, and money.

Paying for advertising on multiple websites is good, but it's not enough and it doesn't guarantee you anything. Third party websites guarantee that they place your book in their email newsletter, they run a promo...but they won't guarantee you anything (90% of them).

There are 5 promotions that I highly recommend for getting results.

BuckBooks - They don't guarantee you anything, but the owner/admin said that you can expect from 50 to 250 sales at

$0.99 and he was right. My first promo had 141 sales, my second 94, my third 101, and my fourth 50.

BooksButterfly - They guarantee a minimum amount of downloads or purchases. If you don't make the minimum number they claim, you will get a prorated refund. I have advertised my Associates book with them and got only 550 downloads just from them and they claimed +1,000. I paid $50 for the promo and got a $25 refund.

BookBub - The *'Holy Grail'* for authors. Every *BookBub* feature is a win and proof that you have achieved a new level of success. Every feature will pay you at least double what you invest in less than 7 days and you get lots of benefits.

EreaderNewsToday - Great feature, great results - $25 for a free book (+1,000 downloads) and $35 for a $0.99 book (+50 sales). I have tried it only once and got 1,100 downloads.

Except these websites, the other ones won't guarantee you anything. So what's the next step in advertising a new book?

'Facebook ads' is the answer.

First of all, to run a Facebook campaign, you need a business page (preferably with your website or blog included) and you should also have an email list ready for getting new subscribers.

Facebook ads allow you to control the daily budget, the cost per click price, and you can select your audience. You basically can control everything.

It's highly recommended to use a low cost per click for books priced at $0.99 or $2.99 to generate more clicks and thus, more potential sales. However, breaking even (cost of the ad = revenue) is difficult and you have small chances of achieving this, but it's possible.

A higher bid = you get clicks faster. If you want to invest $200 in 7 days to get those clicks as fast as possible to boost your ranking, then you should bid higher.

I found out that the best way to make money and increase ranking is to use Facebook ads after you launch the book at $0.99.

After you increase the price to $2.99 or more, set a low bid ($0.02 – $0.04/click), set your budget, and wait for the results.

The average click to sale conversion ratio is around 1-3%. If you get 5,000 clicks in 20 days (5000 clicks x $0.02 = $100) and you have a 1% conversion ratio => 50 sales at $2.99. That equals to 50 sales x 2.07 = $103.50, so you got your money back.

If you use this strategy while the book is priced at $0.99, you would get more sales because of the low price and high bid, but you will lose money on the short-term as you only get only 35% royalty ($0.35/sale). Applying this strategy has a different purpose – ranking the book high enough until you get organic sales (less than #1,000 paid rank).

Even though Facebook is a great way to generate more sales and to increase the ranking of your books on Amazon, it isn't the smartest way to direct people directly to your sales page (like I did in my first ad).

We need to understand that people who are online on Facebook don't look for buying stuff, they are just wasting time, they're chatting with their friends and family, they're looking at photos, news, they're reading articles, or they're looking for a new possible relationship (by adding new people, etc.). So, very few people will be interested in buying a product directly from your ad.

I want to share my experience from my Facebook ads for self-publishing.

I did the following experiment:

I have created an ad for my book, *Kindle Publishing PRO,* for 24 hours with a maximum budget of $10.

The bid I used was $0.1/click at first, then I changed it to $0.03 and the click rate decreased 3 times. I then changed it again to $0.07 and left it like that for the rest of the day.

I was hoping to see at least 1 sale for my book but I didn't. Instead of receiving a sale, I received 144 likes for my Facebook Page *'Entrepreneur Enhanced'*, over 250 likes for the ad, over 340 people were engaged, 2,500+ people saw my ad (impressions), 1 person shared the ad (special thanks to that person for helping me out without knowing me), and 26 people clicked on the ad.

In total, I spent less than $5 for the ad, and I was pleased with the results, even though I didn't break even. It's really a small fee.

The conclusion is this: The wise self-publisher or entrepreneur would use Facebook ads to lead people to a free guide, a newsletter to win their email address, their name, and, of course, their trust. From there, you can sell them your books or you can launch your books better by sending them an email with your new $0.99 offer. Results would be much greater.

I'm pretty sure that if I gave them something for free in exchange for their emails, I would have made more than 50-100 subscribers in one day with only $5, so that would convert into $0.10–$0.30/per new subscriber.

Now, a new problem will appear here. If you use the CPC (bid for 1 click) at $0.05, there will be a lot more people who will click on the ad if they see *"***FREE*** Content – Get your copy now!"*, so the best piece of advice that I can give you is to switch the paying method, which is CPM (cost per impressions – you will be charged in average $0.20 – $0.30/1,000 impressions). As you would expect, using the CPM will significantly decrease the price per new subscriber – it will be somewhere around $0.05 – $0.10/subscriber, which is a complete bargain.

Experts claim that social media is one of the best ways to grow your email list and trust in front of people.

A long time ago, this was not possible and it was way harder to succeed in businesses based on email marketing.

Facebook ads are much better than paying for advertising on different websites. However, to launch a book properly, you need to use all the tools available.

The same story with the ads is available for the Amazon ads. The difference here is that people who are on Amazon are specifically looking to buy something and they have their credit cards ready for purchasing.

I don't know why, but people like to bid at high rates to get quick results and they lose money because they don't know what they're actually doing.

The lowest bid that Amazon allows authors to use is $0.02/click. Same story = $100/$0.02 = 5,000 clicks x 1% conversion ration = 50 sales = $103.50.

Now don't get me wrong, these results vary from book to book (cover, reviews, topic, and title are crucial), but using ads will allow you to grow.

The greatest takeaway from these ads is the fact that you will be seeing organic sales after all the promotions and your email list will also grow.

If you have an average sized email list and you also pay a few websites and you also use ads, you will easily exceed 500 sales in 2-3 weeks, which will convert into a large number of organic sales, and thus, into new subscribers, sales of your other books, and, of course, higher profits.

The same strategy can be applied for Twitter, LinkedIn Ads, and GoodReads Ads. Although they're good and they can provide great results, none of them are as cheap, large, and efficient as Facebook or Amazon.

Chapter 9: Facebook Group and Facebook Page

Facebook has the power to rush the growth of any kind of business, especially if it's an online one.

I've just presented you the whole philosophy with Facebook and Amazon ads, now I want to tell you the "second products" of advertising with Facebook.

When you choose to promote a post, a page, a website, or anything else, it's best to have a dedicated Facebook page. This way, people who see your ads will also see your page and will throw an eye at it. If they find it interesting, they will like it and even follow it.

So, guess what you should do to engage even more readers and potential customers? Post new things on your

Facebook page as if it was your second blog (even if you post the same content or similar content to your main blog or website). When people who follow you will see that you post interesting content that can directly help them, you will gain their trust and they will eventually turn into subscribers, loyal followers, and potential customers.

It's all about the value you deliver.

As a self-publisher, you can give away your books for free or with a discount to whoever you want. Create "giveaways" on your Facebook page such as "Buy and review a book (proof required) and I will send you a free book of your choice from my catalog". This is just a small example, you can come up with dozens of ideas and offers – use your creativity.

Now let's get back to our main subject, **launching a book**. Now imagine when you release a new title, a part of the people who are following you on Facebook will look at your new release and some of them will buy it; it's just like an email based business and the best part of this is that it's free.

From creating a page, you can then invite your followers and subscribers (Facebook Page, blog, email list, podcast, etc.) to join your exclusive Secret Facebook Group – share your thoughts and experience with other people like you or who like you. From there, you get even closer to them and you build a strong relationship with loyal followers.

This way, you can allow them to grow, to contact you, to promote your products, to help them promote their products, and all of these for free. You are in full control of the Facebook Page, so you are responsible for who goes in and who goes out.

It's not easy to run all these ideas and tools simultaneously, but it's totally possible.

What you need to understand is that you can build strong connections with people you don't know completely free of charge. Facebook is just one piece of the puzzle, there are other players in this game, too. Research all of them and choose the ones that fit you best.

Other Books By Ryan Stevens

Amazon Associates Affiliate Program

Learn the basics of affiliate marketing, and learn how Amazon Associates works.

Evernote In 90 Minutes Or Less

Organize and de-clutter your daily tasks by installing this free up. A complete tour of the application is included and it's great for beginners.

Kindle Publishing PRO

Learn everything about Kindle Publishing from A to Z – how to upload, how to market, how to write, tips, tricks and more.

Entrepreneur Enhanced

Learn the fundamentals of entrepreneurship and how I managed to start my own business. Strategies, experiences and my own thoughts are all in a nutshell.

CreateSpace Publishing For Independent Self-Publishers

Increase your income from self-publishing by creating print editions of your books. The whole process is free.

Write a Review

Reviews are very important for anyone, especially for people like me who create digital content for readers just like you. To improve the quality of the books and to also improve the readers' experience, reviews are essential.

Let me know in several words what you think, what you liked and what you disliked in this book.

Thanks in advance!

Conclusion

Thank you once again for purchasing and for reading this book, more just like this one on the way.

Subscribe to my email list, follow me on Amazon or simply send me a message or a comment in case you have any questions or suggestions.

Regards,

Ryan

www.ingramcontent.com/pod-product-compliance
Lightning Source LLC
Chambersburg PA
CBHW070908180526
45168CB00005B/1974